CW00447648

THE WEDDING DANCE:

30 Essential Tips

Mônica Harbor

THE WEDDING DANCE   2

*For married people and
those who intend to get
married.*

THE WEDDING DANCE   3

THE WEDDING DANCE   4

CONTENTS

THE WEDDING DANCE   5

1. AFFECTION IS ALMOST EVERYTHING

The very first tip to make the marriage dance pleasurable and lasting is to invest in the long-standing of the dating (or romantic) mood. From the very beginning as a couple, every day and always, partners should demonstrate mutual affection - even when the fire of passion dims as the years go by.

Affection, affection, affection... it's never too much! Be it only a woodpecker's kiss, a run of fingers through the hair, a smile, an unassuming wink, a simple act of kindness- getting them a glass of water before bed, for example.

Of course the old and traditional "I love you" must be decanted any time it comes to us. Even an "*I love you to the moon and back*" is allowed. The important thing is for the other to feel wanted and loved.

I use to welcome waking up with an effusive "Good morning!" and with a smooch on the eye here and there. With both hands I caress Edward's cheeks when the rough patches of his sparse beard are protruding. Speaking of which...

2. THE HANDS

The hands are powerful orchestrating tools for the senses. Despite their dexterity and effectiveness in love games, especially in the penumbra, the hands have great power in broad daylight. To walk side-by-side holding hands is fundamental. The warmth of entwined hands heats up the relationship. Everytime they touch, an unusual bond is forged.

Even the otters know this (type up "otters holding hands"

on Youtube), but there are a
lot of human couples who seem
to not know of this simple and
powerful linkage.

I like to hold Edward's
hand while the traffic light is
red and he (or I) frees it from
the steering wheel. I take
advantage of this moment for
another meeting of hands that,
immediately, connects our
souls.

3. THE OTHERS ARE JUST THE OTHERS AND THAT'S IT

When we choose someone to share a lifetime together, that someone must become the most important person to us. Neither children nor parents may claim the top spot in our attention's podium.

Parents and children are our treasure, blood of our blood, owners of our unconditional love. But children grow up and find their own soulmates and raise their own families. Our parents deserve our immense gratitude and support, but they've already lived (or are still living) their own romances. Now it's our time.

For a relationship to be truly solid, our partner must be our deepest longing, our greatest accomplice in this journey called life. It's mainly with them that we share our joy and pain while dealing with life.

Together, holding hands, we will take care of our children, support our parent's

old age and, above all, love
each other.

4. CHEATING… IS ONLY A MATTER OF BEGINNING

The world if full of pretty, talented, charismatic, attractive people. You can't hope for a person like that to slip by unnoticed. The beautiful, elegant and charming must be recognized, but we shouldn't let those pseudo-princes (and princesses) take over our minds and become objects of our desire.

Edward and I face the beautiful with naturalness. When we meet an Apollo or Venus de Milo, we tell each other something along these lines: "So-and-so is handsome, but you're also very much so". Which is not untrue, since hidden beneath a well sculpted body or a brilliant mind, there are imperfections, ugliness, vices, and manias that we haven't the slightest idea of.

To exchange our loved one, the one that hand-in-hand chose us to build a life as a couple, is a signal of immaturity, fickleness and disrespect with the other partner, to say the least.

As cheating implies lying, dissimulation, tensions,

fears, it will take a huge toll on the cheater's emotional side. If the cheater is caught - which always is - sadness and unhappiness from from someone who've bet all their chips on him will follow. It's rather more decent and intelligent to invest on the marriage, renew it, make different things that may fire up past attraction.

Oh, how wonderful it is to trust and to be worthy of trusting! The lovers will be gifted with a powerful sensation of comfort, safety and love. And this feeling will maximize all other good dimensions of life.

And it's no use thinking that cheating only once is no big deal. It is! The burden will remain forever. Not to mention the fact that cheating is only a matter of beginning.

5. A LIE HAS NO LEGS

One of the essential moves of the marriage dance is called sincerity. Being honest and truthful with our dancing partner may be kind of hard for many of us, but to live dissimulating and manipulating is far more complex and risky, not to mention, fatal.

Dancers that use to lie, sooner or later, will be unmasked and will lose their partner's credibility and admiration. The immediate gifts that lying can bring are not worth the embarrassment and disappointment that will soon follow. If a lie has no legs, it surely has no place in the marriage dance.

Be wary, however, of the exacerbation of impressions. There are spouses who are "sincericidal" and will always fire "truths" nonstop. Do you really need to tell your partner everyday that he is fat and big-bellied, that his mother is a pain in the ass, that the food he cooked with so much love is horrible? Even if, to the sniper, these perceptions are true, he must develop a sense of opportunity,

with the possible consequence
of undermining her partner's
self-esteem.

6. SOMEONE HAS TO COMPROMISE

Just like in dancing, even the more legitimate and attuned couples will eventually stumble, and misunderstanding is going to be inevitable. We are talking about human beings, full of flaws, whims and bringing diverse family and cultural values, sometimes irreconcilable, in their baggage. Everything is very prone to disagreement, confrontation, resentment. In those moments, it's not possible to keep on waltzing as if nothing else is happening.

And when in heated confrontational mood, dialogue becomes impossible. A full brake must be applied to the dancing, that is, getting away from the critical scene, in a way that you can take a deep breath and make the blood stop boiling. Only after the dust has settled, one of the two must take the initiative in search for a possible compromise, a solution that concurs to the well-being of both sides.

It's not that easy! Somebody must compromise a bit

more in some circumstances. But it is important for the beneficiary to develop a sense of justice so that, in future quarrels, whoever compromised in the last time is compensated.

In this area it's crucial not to quibble over trifles. Don't throw a tantrum over whims! If we think about it, most impasses revolve around unimportant matters that we want to impose in our self interest, that is, for egoism and picking on the other.

Edward and I usually compromise with no further delay, one of us always steps forward and compromises without beating around the bush. Now, when something is really important to one of us, it's enough that they verbalize: "*This is very important to me*". That's it! In our code of conduct, this is the magic password for the other to give up their whims and compromise without throwing a fit.

7. FORGIVE THEM

Dropping the ball (or stepping on the other's feet) is human. Sometimes a spouse makes a mistake, a mistake that displeases and, sometimes, hurts the other partner. In this case, the doer must unmistakably admit the fault and take it over with courage and commitment to repair it, for him to be worthy of forgiveness.

This way, noticing the sincerity and recognition, the other must mentalize the virtues and good moments they've spent together accept the repenting one with arms wide open. The doer must, in his turn, take the commitment not to repeat the same mistake.

Edward and I have a rule not to sleep upset with each other. We always find a way to reconcile.

Of course, if the incidents get worse and there's no real commitment to repair them, really think if it's not time to send your partner dancing... alone.

8. WALKING ON EGGSHELLS

There are days in which a spouse wakes up in a bad mood or, after a bad hair day, comes home stressed. It's one of the two: either the other avoids any situations that may worsen his partner's mood - walking on eggshells - or risks dialogue and let her give vent, trying not to absorb the acid discharge that he will receive. How hard it is!...

The important thing is not to take part in that frenetic dance of exasperation, after all, "two owls don't kiss".

When I notice Edward is irritated, I try to stay calm and help him in any way. If it's not possible, I avoid further reaching out. I imagine all the jumping through hoops he must have done in those remote days that I had PMS...

The fact is that no one deserves bad moods and ill-temper!

9. THE DRIVER IS THE BOSS

At the beginning of our marriage, we used to stress ourselves out when, in the car, we disagreed on the route to follow or where to park. I had my favorite routes to get somewhere, Edward had his. I prefered a parking spot, he said he prefered some other. And because of these minor choices, sometimes we argued and got upset with one another.

Then one day we had a pitched battle because of that

when I was driving. I stopped the car abruptly and screamed: - I won't drive with you trying to drive for me anymore! If you want so, drive! - I ordered. I stepped out, got in the passenger seat, he took the driver seat while I was giving vent to my irritation.

After getting coolheaded, we decided that, from that moment on, whoever was at the steering wheel gets to decide everything. In other words, the route and parking place would be exclusive calls of the one driving. After that, we've never had any other arguments in that matter.

And oh, we've also arranged that whoever is not driving may give a suggestion, but the driver chooses freely if he will take the advice or not. And whoever suggested must not feel resented if the suggestion was declined.

On a day to day basis, in the car, we avoid sticking our oars in each other's driving preferences.

10. IN PUBLIC, ONLY PRAISE

It always bothers me when I witness a spouse publicly criticizing his loved one. It's humiliating for the victim of the criticism and awkward for whoever is watching the scene.

I believe that whoever stoops to something like that is an insecure, immature partner and ignorant on the matters of love and how to treat people. Deluded, believing he is doing something great exhibiting publicly his moral superiority over his partner, the wrongdoer is, on the contrary, exhibiting an unmatched level of ugliness and inelegance.

If not to manifest compliments in public, the dancing partner should hold back his criticism, reproaches and ironies and find a way to work around those deplorable and childish mannerisms. Whereas the partner who is the victim of the show-off-critic should call her wrongdoer in private and tell him clearly that she doesn't like it, or better yet, finds that attitude inadmissible.

It's necessary for the victim to put her foot down and demand an attitude worthy of a balanced couple that respects each other in private and in public.

11. JEALOUSY, ENVY, COMPETITION

I believe that all couples that are still together have survived some coarse moments, especially some related to jealousy, envy and competition. These are some feelings that use to plague young couples (or old, immature ones), who still haven't conquered plenitude in the relationship.

When one partner (or both) let these vile feelings to take over, it's like drinking a cup full of poison and pouring cold water on the relationship. With a shaken self-esteem, the jealous person projects his insecurity onto the other and transfers his fears and insecurities. What lies beneath jealousy is over-the-top attachment. The fear of losing your partner's love.

The jealous person wishes to be, exclusively, the other's center of attention. He suffers when he notices the other's interest in other people (or projects), fears losing her deliriously. Based on that fear, the jealous one starts to develop strange, poisoned, jagged attitudes. Instead of sharing her moment of pleasure and achievement and learn alongside her, the jealous person wants to compete in a destructive way . That's where the danger lies!

I know it's not easy to reprogram feelings. Imperfection is intrinsic to our human condition. It's a huge challenge, but not an insurmountable one.

I suggest that the jealous one seek help from true friends and therapists. But, above all, to search within for the values and wonders that made his partner choose him in a sea of people available in the ballroom of life. If you feel like you are falling short of your partner's expectations, better yourself, renew yourself, and of course, find dialogue and complicity in your partner. Dialogue is the solution's starting point.

12. THE DREADED RELATIONSHIP DISCUSSION

Discussing the relationship is a trump card that usually make men scared. But we women must not give up that powerful resource to retake the dance, when our footwork is starting to frequently get out of synch with our partner's.

It's time to face differences, expose feelings, settle doubts, align expectations. Avoiding prejudgement, guilt, resentment, irony, it's time to talk face to face in search for each other's truth, to refind the relationship foundations and re-establish adrift agreements.

So this moment of truth works as a brake so that the marriage dance goes back to being fluid and a source of pleasure.

13. A SOUND MIND IN A SOUND BODY

A lasting relationship requires a lasting life, a lasting life requires taking care of the body and soul's health. An appropriate diet, physical activity, regular medical *check ups*, personal projects and leisure time are the basics.

And you don't need to be a Brad Pitt or Angelina Jolie, but it's important to be fit. Don't get sloppy! A little bit of vanity is healthy (and seductive), and this goes without saying, but don't go overboard. Elegance is everything!

Trying to balance the body workout (walks, sports, pilates, going to the gym) and the brain/emotional workout (reading, going to the movies, music, having a social life, therapy etc) with other life activities is a good challenge to be pursued.

And each one must be the other's greatest encourager and accomplice in this goal of a healthy mind and body. One's

well-being must be a reason for
the other's contentment.

14. IN SICKNESS AND IN HEALTH

Many of us forget the vows we made at the altar, with the blessings of God and men, when we made the commitment to "be true in good times and in bad, in sickness and in health".

The mishaps, the disappointments, the sickness are inherent to life, of course, and are always haunting couples and demanding that they comply with the wedding vows.

Even with all the health care in the world, we can still fall ill, be it physically or psychologically. It's precisely at times like these that love is put to the test.

Taking care of a sick spouse requires dedication, renouncing, giving yourself, which may lead to fatigue, to pain, to the desire of getting away - why not admit it? But the marriage kit establishes the commitment, that once overcome, will strengthen the relationship even more. At these critical times, seek help of family and close friends.

The key takeaway is to treat your partner the way you would want to be treated.

15. SOMEWHERE IN TIME

The wedding photo album is a precious witness of the great union. The beautiful and happy moments are documented and available to be relived in the memory.

I like to keep our wedding album close at hand. Nowadays it sits in the central table in the living room. When we lie down on the sofa unpretentiously, now and then, we open our album and admire that young pair of sweethearts (ourselves) who chose to share life as a couple. At those moments, we usually go through our milestones and ups and downs and celebrate the fact that we are still together today.

16.WHERE ARE WE GOING?

Which movie should we watch? In which restaurant will we have lunch on Sunday? Doubts like these pop up frequently when couples decide to unwind. Leisure time should be decided with fun and lightness, but that doesn't always happen.

Deciding, for example, which movie to watch is not always that easy. Men tend to prefer action movies in general, and of course, the more bloodshed the better. We women, for the most part, prefer intelligent, sensible, romantic movies. Finding a happy medium between those two extremes is almost always a good challenge. Sometimes there will be a little frustration for those involved.

Thus, Edward and I agreed to alternate between who chooses what to watch. This has worked pretty well, but I must confess that I'm more intolerant towards his movies. After all, no one deserves "The Fantastic Four", "Mad Max" and "X-Men: Apocalypse". On these occasions, I would turn my "screensaver" on and pretend to be watching them...

Nowadays we are more authentic. When it's a movie that I don't really care for, I'll stay close by, but do and think about something else (he also does that), without any pretending.

About the restaurants, we usually find something that pleases both of us. Besides, Edward and I are the kind of couple that like going to our favorite restaurant multiple times.

17. COMINGS AND GOINGS... TO THE MALL

Apart from the inherent convergences of human nature and culture, men and women tend to exhibit divergent propensities. One of them is the act of going to the mall.

Edward and I already strained ourselves in our goings to the mall. He has no patience with window-shopping - one habit I love doing, without ever buying anything. Edward doesn't really get it. He thinks you should only spend time looking at shop windows if you have a real intention of buying something.

That's why whenever we went to the mall together, one (or both) got frustrated. He got tired of my disposition to window-shop with seemingly no objective; As for me, I knew he wasn't digging it and ended up suppressing my look-at-everything-buy-nothing instincts. The result: I avoid going to shopping malls with Edward. I prefer to go alone or with a friend, it's so much more fun!

Nowadays we only go to the mall together if we have a

clear objective on what to do
(movies, theater, restaurant,
an exhibition) or shopping for
something specific.

18. OPINION OR REINFORCEMENT?

This tip should have been written by Edward. It's him who is constantly boasting to his friends about how to deal with women when we ask an opinion on clothing, shoes or jewellery, for example.

According to Edward, a man should not honestly manifest his opinion when he is asked about her looks. To him, on such occasions, he runs the risk of expressing an opinion that's the opposite of what she wants to hear. Edward adds: in reality, when she asks for your opinion, she just wants reinforcement, a reaffirmation of her choice.

Edward says jokingly that, at those moments, the man should pretend to analyze the situation, but should really try to find out what she already decided and compliment it vehemently, so she feels satisfied and safe. I find Edward's tip a bit questionable, but I do recognize that the marriage dance has its subterfuges. But

just in case, I decided to
write it down...

19. WHO WILL DO THE DISHES?

Back in my mother's day, women were responsible for housework, from cleaning and organizing the house, to cooking, including washing the dishes. It's was up to the man to work outside, and provide the family with financial support. Today that labour division makes no sense. Women have taken the streets and are as much part of the workforce as men. It wouldn't be fair for them to still bear the burden of all household chores.

This way, each couple should split household chores as evenly as possible. Each case should be treated differently. If one of them is feeling burned out by working outside, the other should take in a bit more of the housework weight. If both work outside in the same proportion, then household chores should be evenly split. For example, if someone cooks dinner, the other should do the dishes. If one does the laundry, the other should mop the floor. If one fixes the car, the other does the shopping. And so on and so forth.

In my house, Edward and I are more inclined to do specific chores. He handles money, investments, redemptions, bank transfers, payments, because he is more keen on financial matters, besides shopping the most. It's I who schedule appointments, deal with the cleaning lady, electricians, plumbers and order things to get fixed.

The main point is to not overburden both parties. When our children were younger, I was the most invested in their education, but I do recognize that Edward was far more dedicated to work than I was.

20. LOVE IS EXPENSIVE

Another concrete aspect of living as a couple is having the financial means to support the lifestyle of both involved. Married people need a home of their own - as the old saying goes! A home needs an infrastructure to get equipped, maintained and supplied with all kinds of items, food, rent, electricity, clothing etc. All of that revolves around money.

It follows that the couple must, before getting married, find work and resources to support household necessities, besides entertainment, education, health, a whole heap of stuff.

When they are strapped for cash, the couple must square their accounts and adjust their lifestyle so they don't get in debt. Running after or from creditors is a poison to the relationship. I know people who, in the verge of a financial crisis, instead of cutting costs, keep spending as if nothing had happened and demand from their partner a magic solution

In such situations, the only way is rolling up your

sleeves and finding jobs that can reestablish old comfort levels. These are some of the reasons why, even in fat years it is essential to avoid squandering and to save all you can for the lean years.

Edward and I went through a delicate time when he lost his job. Together, we faced the crisis and could keep the dancing going, without letting the ball drop.

21. FRIENDS, FRIENDS

In our early years of marriage, we had some setbacks due to friendships. I was more sociable than Edward, and so, I had more friends in my social baggage than him. I wanted to keep my bachelorette's years gang the same, but the marriage's obligations ended up dissipating that Utopia.

With time, we end up being more selective and seek out those friends who overcame the new situation and won the heart and mind of our spouse.

This is the simple way we've found to conciliate friendships and marriage, without further jumping through hoops

Of course we have that group of girl friends, which we can count on our fingers and toes that, independently of our hubby liking them, we preserve and still meet up periodically - preferably when he is doing other things and won't miss us.

Pay attention: be careful not to encourage intimate proximity between friends of the opposite sex, in a confidant-like way. It's not unusual for some role confusion to happen: the relationship between friends could be misinterpreted and may set up undesired romantic feelings for someone involved. It's better to be on the safe side...

22. CHILDREN? IF WE DON'T HAVE THEM, HOW CAN WE KNOW?

Nowadays I see a lot of childfree couples. They want exclusivity to live their love life without the burdens of fatherhood and motherhood. I respect their choice, especially because they don't know what it means to have children.

Having children is the greatest proof of love a couple can ever have. It is, without a doubt, the greatest project a couple can do together. It is the inexorable physical and psychological union of their existences. A couple with children will be forever bonded, for better and for worse.

But we have to admit: a child is an earthquake that will shake the couple's relationship in such a way that it will demand so much more than what we have said until now. In other words, if dancing as a couple already requires a high level of mindfulness so as not to stumble over, try to picture dancing with three, four, five people… It's definitely no walk in the park! An expanded mind and sane body will be necessary to rise to the occasion and, of course, more love, more renunciation, more dedication, more work, more money, more of everything.

But that is the natural law of the human species and, I believe, we can only reach life's plenitude when we experience parenthood. Children are our big bet for the future. They are the guardians of what's best in us (sometimes of what's worst). Our DNA and our values are printed on our offspring cells, which they will pass on to the future for our grandchildren, for our great-grandchildren and that is the way we attach ourselves and perpetuate our existences and love. However, educating children is a herculean task that will require books and more books and will never be truly finished.

In any case, there's a premise that I wouldn't forget to mention for the couple's own well-being: children are sacred and deserving of all of our love and dedication. However they came after, and the relationship should not come second. On the contrary, the spouses' love and positive complicity should prevail.

I know men and women who, when they have a baby, become so dazzled with parenthood that they forget to nurture their relationship. They become distant and start seeing their partner as an outsider, a nuisance, if not a burden. The promises of love, affection and happiness are forgotten. And that is certainly dangerous ground...

Unknown to these mothers and fathers is the fact that their children will grow up, relegate their friends, their sweethearts and spouses, and then they, the parents, will come second. And it's not that their children are evil or ungrateful. It is just the natural course of life.

We should obviously do the best we can to nurture our children, but always standing shoulder to shoulder with our partner. In this path, we support each other, and laugh and cry together.

Knowing this, let's not waste time nor love to bestow upon our dancing partner.

23. YOUR, MY AND OUR FAMILY

Family is the basis, the ground, the reference inside each of us. However complicated it is, we still hold love and responsibility towards it. Our parents grow old and need our attention and affection until the end of their days. More often than not, it involves hands-on and financial support.

It may happen that the family - including siblings - of one dancing partner is more needy than the other's family.

In this case it will require more attention and, sometimes, more resources. This may bring about a certain unbalance, since the couple is investing more in one side, tilting the scale. This will take a fair amount of comprehension and generosity to support your partner, because, after all, he can't deny that to his original family.

Furthermore, what goes around comes around, and sometime your original family may also need it. If you supported your partner in taking care of his family, he will probably return the favor and come in useful when yours is in need. The old saying "one hand washes the other (and both wash the face)" works perfectly here.

But if the washing back doesn't occur, with tact and in a subtle way, it won't hurt to remind him, and please, you don't have to rub it in. Helping each others family should be done, as far as possible, willingly. In the end, a proof of love shouldn't be imposed, it should be done spontaneously.

24. TOGETHER IN THE SAME DIRECTION

Let's fix Saint-Exupéry's quote just a bit: "Love does ~~not~~ (yes it does) consist of gazing at each other, but (it consists, above all), in looking outward together in the same direction."

Contemplation and romanticism are desirable attitudes in a relationship, but they are not enough. For it to be harmonious and lasting, you have to nurture mutual goals. It is evident that children are enough of a mutual goal, but like we've already said, there will come a day when they take wings and leave the nest. In that moment, if the couple didn't take the time to develop other projects and interests, the relationship could go awry.

That's why it is advisable to cultivate spaces for only the both of you - without forgetting your individuality and your own projects. Besides sex, which is intimate, pleasurable and exclusive, the habit of going to the movies must be kept, promoting a special day for a romantic dinner, sharing

readings, talking about
politics, soccer, religion,
traveling to stunning places
that are the dream of both
partners, doing charity as a
team, and of course, walking
together in the same
direction,, holding hands...

25.JOINING TOOTHBRUSHES

After the honeymoon, nothing like routine to make the discrepancies between two different beings who have diverse habits and idiosyncrasies, who decided to put their toothbrushes together, stand out. A lot of these differences are valued by the other person. The others, however, are such a disconcerting antagonism, unnerving, even.

For every couple, there's always a partner who is more

organized. Someone who methodically puts every piece of clothing in the dirty laundry basket, while the other leaves them anywhere, maybe even on the floor. Someone who caps the toothpaste and religiously leaves it on the same place, while the other, in addition to not capping it, usually forgets it on the TV or by the computer. Someone who never loses the car keys, while the other has a hard time on a daily basis finding it. To this type of person, smartphones, wallets, pens and other accessories seem to have legs of their own, because they are never in the place where they left them, and furthermore, these objects mysteriously hide themselves.

The tidy one, in his turn, is obnoxious, because he is unable to relax and to eventually let go a reasonable mess. Even when tired, he insists on organizing everything now, leaving nothing for later. When it comes to the crunch, he is too proud to give himself a break from folding shirts and putting them in the drawer. Usually it's this person who worries if the door is locked – sometimes they will check that detail more than once.

The sloppy one, poor thing, usually receives endless classes on organization and method. Every so often she is reprimanded and asked for things way beyond her possibilities. When the tidy one buys organizing gadgets, the sloppy one will only toy with them for a day and no longer see their usefulness. However, when the methodical one needs a document that he carefully put away in his briefcase and can't find it, he already knows what (in fact, who) happened...

After the initial bumpy road, the intelligent couple will circumvent those differences, but someone always ends up making their habits more flexible, so the tidy one, for the sake of the family, allows room for some disorganization and the sloppy one tries getting into the system. In this case there is a healthy accommodation, in which both sides compromise for a better way to live together. Yet, one inch of intransigence is enough for the conflicts to last forever, until death (or divorce) do them part.

26. THE GREATEST RIVAL

Nowadays, the biggest rival of the couple is not a fancy man or woman. The greatest rival is everywhere: on the bed, on the kitchen's table, on the sofa, in the toilet, in the car, on the table of a bar, in the movies, in church, in the elevator... It is it who steals Edward from me the most. It is relentless and seductive, and has many tricks in its sleeve to keep us captives. And it is so successful at doing it!...

Sometimes, when I try talking to Edward, he is so hypnotized by the cunning rival that he doesn't even listen to me.

Edward was the first to bring the small and multifunctional rival between us. In the beginning I was jealous and got annoyed with Edward's attachment, but in the end I accepted the love triangle, and out of the blue, I also got involved with one of my own, thus forming a love rectangle.

The truth is that, if we are not careful, we will be co-opted and sink under the infinite possibilities of the small smartphone, especially when surrounded by the social networks (*whatsapp, Facebook* and similar things). Oh, how powerful it is!...

I try not to use the cell phone when Edward is near. He even tries it too, but doesn't resist the callings of the small gadget. As an act of protest, now and then, when he is typing in front of me, I open a book or a newspaper so he can notice how distant we are at times like that...

Still, even as a rival, there is a code of ethics which should be incorporated into the love rectangle: the cell phone is a private gadget, and in respect of the other's individuality, should not be snooped into. I can even look at his smartphone's content, if he invites me or lets me do so (and vice-versa). The couple's trust and respect goes through those small living together agreements.

27. HONEY, I'M HOME!

With that exclamation, Earl, protagonist of the TV series "Dinosaurs" informed his spouse, Fran, that he'd just arrived from work.

Along those lines, it doesn't matter if I'm tired, sad, stressed; when I come home, my small dog Sebastian comes hastily and grants me an over-the-top greeting. This way, he leaves me with no room for gloom and grumpiness.

The advice for whoever is coming home or whoever is there

already is to greet the partner inspired in these characters. Arriving with enthusiasm simply because you are back is a wonderful way to meet your partner, every day, if possible. Welcoming an arriving person with arms wide open is a gift, a good omen for great moments together.

28. LITTLE ACTS OF KINDNESS

Daily life is full of opportunities for us to make little acts of kindness for our partner, like: surprising him with a nice breakfast on the table; covering him with a blanket when he is sleeping with no covers; closing blinds so he can sleep a little longer; opening the elevator door for him; letting him get the first and the last piece of the delicious cake we are sharing; offering him a ride when he needs it; bringing home some treats that he loves; and gifting him a glass of water at any time of the day.

These and other little acts show that lovingness and kindness are small but great acts to win someone's heart.

29. SPOONING

Sleeping together is the most important moment for the couple. At that time, the lovers are by themselves, body and mind sprawled on the bed with the feeling of another day gone by. It is time to relax and find a comfortable position to spend the night. Each couple must find their own sleeping arrangement, in a way to obtain a restorative slumber, and if possible, establish contact.

Edward and I soon found the spooning position to nestle

up against each other. He is the big spoon behind me. To us, that is the perfect position! Our bodies are interlocked in such a way that I feel protected and warmed, not to mention how wonderful it is to feel his body against mine. And since Edward is the more hot-natured one, we always find a position in bed that favours the ventilation on his back. It's such a delight!

If you haven't tried it yet, you're wasting time...

30. SHALL WE TALK ABOUT SEX?

The intimate relationship between two lovers is something sacred and secret. It's not nice to go out there and spill the beans about what's going on in the alcove. Whoever does that is seen as indiscreet or an exhibitionist. That's why you shouldn't expect me to tell what are our favorite sex positions, or how many times we have sex per week, let alone how long it takes for him to get an orgasm and stuff like that.

But I must say that sex is, in a lot of ways, consequence of the couples' ups and downs - keep in mind the previous advice. The more you love outside of bed, the more you love in it. It's like foreplay already started with the "Honey, I'm home!". Everything converges to the climax in bed. Though I do think that men are less sensible to external factors, while women are much more impacted by them.

Yet something specific must be said: men tend to

demand sex more than women do. They don't need many stimuli or reasons to get locked and loaded. Women are more susceptible to the context, to the inside and outside appeals - having a TV and phones in the bedroom don't help. It follows that some women use that classic excuse to not have sex: "I have a headache." The worst thing is, that sometimes this is true...

When the woman doesn't have the conditions or is not willing to, the advice is to not let the man pleasure himself solo. She can interact with his body, caress him and give him a hand so that he can have pleasure in a more interactive way.

Any way, libido should be enjoyed within the outskirts of home, so there will be no desire left for the lover to look at other skirts and two-time... After all, as the old adage goes: "an empty sack cannot stand upright".

On the other side, as time passes, the inevitable changes in men and women's bodies can be seem, and they need to be openly exposed so that the couple can circumvent and it and find a new rhythm for the dancing that is appropriate to the new situation.

With menopause, for example, vaginal lubrication is fairly reduced. It is then necessary to ask a gynecologist for guidance, who will prescribe creams and lubricants to preserve pleasure and avoid pain during intercourse. Men, in turn, may need stimuli to maintain focus. Obviously a touch of creativity and boldness will augment the choreography.

The main thing is for each lover to express themselves in the search for the satisfaction of the needs (and fantasies) of the other, and of course, of herself.

After reviewing these dance steps so many times, I felt like practicing some of them with Edward. Right now he is in bed watching TV. I will soon run my fingers through his hair and hold our hands together…

And you, what are you waiting for? Find your partner and get to work...

Printed in Great Britain
by Amazon

14983699R00059